Solo the Clown

was with and without
wherever and whenever
without a doubt
happily contented
inside and out
he is whole
body and soul

Cover and Illustration by Michelle Aguis

Nothing Matters

Live Every Moment

❧

Richard Grant

Acknowledgements

To Lao and Walter Russell, for setting up The University Of Science And Philosophy at Waynesboro, Virginia USA. They have written many books individually and collectively, most importantly the *Home Study Course*, (HSC) which has enabled me to come to grips with Who I Am

Also I would like to acknowledge Glen Clarke for his book, *The Man Who Tapped The Secrets Of The Universe* which is a wonderful book about Walter Russell.

To Yasuhiko Kimura, and his book, *Think Kosmically Act Globally*.

To Unity School Of Christianity.

Consciousness Unfolding by Joel S Goldsmith.

The Sermon On The Mount by Emmet Fox.

Second Edition December 2004

Enquiries regarding any form of reproduction beyond the above permissions should be directed to the publisher.

Richard Grant
12/81 High St
Southport QLD 4215 Australia
(07) 55640634
Email: rgrant@qldnet.com.au

Foreword

The purpose in the writing of this book is to clarify with my own self the awakening that has taken place within me. The abundant energy I enjoy, as I learn to obey the Natural Law of Balance, I can have the power of Mind to command Nature and my own life. For Mind is Universal, God's mind and my mind are one.

To me the most exciting scientific fact in my evolution and progress in the world today, is to awaken the Creative Force within me, to the creative ideas, which gets rid of human frailties, beliefs, doubt, fear, disease, sin. This brings healing and freedom of truth.

To those who read this book, may not understand any of it, or agree with what I have written. But it may trigger off what they already know that they didn't know they knew.

Chapter One

THE AWAKENING

All my life I knew that there was more to life than what I was experiencing, I could not find the answers to but why. Having lived the life of the prodigal son for so long, separate from God, I was an ideal manger for The Christ to be born in, as I came to awaken to the Kingdom of Heaven was within me. Then it dawned on me that the answers were within me, opened up a whole new way of thinking, as I looked at my purpose for being here this lifetime.

I then started to question my beliefs, for they had been a very limiting force for too long. My spiritual path has been dominated by my ego, which took me deeper into the illusion and further away from my true beingness. My beliefs were all fear based, every one of them. Love and fear cannot coexist. Lately doors have opened up like crazy, triggering off within me what I already knew but didn't know that I knew. It's not what I am reading in books that are of interest, but what is being triggered within me, which is a whole new way of thinking. I

❧

Jesus said:

Come sit with me for awhile and let me help you see as I see, to feel the depth of the spirit in you, as I have felt it in me, let me show the way, the high road, let me lead you into the wonderful world of Christ within you, where you will know, and know that you know, that you are a limitless expression of the infinite, and I can assure you that when you realize the truth as I have realized it, you will be able to do all the things that I have done, and even greater things will you do.

❧

now realize this life is a never ending process of awakening, which makes it very exciting, as I let go and let God shine through.

When I feel a need or a want for anything, this has a balancing and opposite effect on the inner, which creates a feeling of lack, and imbalance within. This is fear, based of not having enough; this in turn limits me. All my life, being a typical male, I was only interested in two things, my belly and what hung beneath it. I could not get enough to eat, and I could never get enough sex. This would have created an enormous lack within, which would have caused my body a lot of turmoil, limiting me in every way.

I feel what one must learn comes from within, it's an acquired state of being, I feel each person's awakening will occur in his or her own time and own way when he or she is ready for it. Also I feel this stuff cannot be taught; it's an acquired consciousness, which needs to be lived. Anybody who thinks they can teach another the way they should go, is covering up their own faults. This is the way of the ego.

It has taken me fifty years to fully come to grips with a statement that our father made. It was at a family gathering, which was held every Sunday morning, that he said to us nine children, and to all those who normally turned up to the Sunday family gathering.

"You know if I told you blokes how simple life was, you

❧

On a bus one day, I sat next to a youth of decidedly hippie appearance. He was wearing one shoe.

"I see you have lost a shoe," I ventured.

"No, man, I have found one," he replied.

❧

would only laugh at me."

"No, come on tell us dad, what is it?"

"Well, good and God is the same word, so we need only to think good thoughts, if you feel a need to exercise, deep breathing will suffice. Then nothing else matters." He also said, "It's our duty to influence our fellow man as we walk down the street by knowing who we are."

I now realize that one good thought will uplift the whole race, as does one drop of water raise the whole ocean.

The title to this book came to me when I realized that 'I And the Father are one'. My understanding of God is that my body is in my soul, and my soul in the 'One Mind', which is God, or my Christ Consciousness. To me Jesus was the way shower, and Christ is the conscious mind of God within. If more time had been spent on teaching what Jesus came to tell us, instead of worshiping him I feel I would have been able to understand where he was coming from much sooner in my life.

The inner mind not only shows us the solution to any problem and the right direction to take in any situation, but being the universal Mind, it is the consciousness of every individual, and brings every person and circumstance together for the good of the whole. This creates an enormous amount of energy, which is what Jesus meant when he said we could move the mountains to the sea, and much much more. True Love, or unconditional love can only be experienced from the Christ

"I must learn to know Nature spiritually as the living expression of the Universal Thinker. For there can be no loss or hurt to any unit of Nature, even if life itself be the cost, for any service given to any part by any part must be given to the whole."

Walter Russell, Divine Iliad

conscious level where all is one.

My beingness is not in my body; it is in the One Mind, which is where God is. In the same way love is also in the Christ Consciousness. The Father within gives me love as a gift, in the degree that I re-give it this completes and voids the cycle, so that it may be repeated. The same thing with energy, which comes from the desire to express with joy and ecstasy, and providing I don't identify with the effect more will be given for me to re-give. This becomes habit forming as I awaken to who I really am.

> "*The perpetuity of Creation is based upon the constant giving of one half of a cycle to the other half for the purpose of repeating the creative process through another cycle of giving for re-giving.*"
>
> From *The Divine Iliad*, by Walter Russell

For me this is the Universal Law of Love. This takes a fair bit of coming to grips with, it means that the fulcrum has been moved one step toward the Father, this takes it away from the ego self, instead of thinking that Love came from me, Richard, and I expressed it out in the material world. The fulcrum is now between the Father, who is one half the cycle and Richard being a fulcrum for the other half in his expression into the material world. For every action there is an opposite and opposing reaction, which is cause and effect, the law of balance every thought has an opposite opposing effect from the inner to the outer, or the outer to the inner. It is instantaneous. Or 'I Am' a

❧

The beauty is not in the rose or the magic forest, beauty is within us as we express the universe of who we are.

❧

divine, immortal, invisible soul, centered in a physical body made up of thought waves of motion, which is centered in the mass consciousness of all that is, which I call God. Or Spirit. The I Am is never created. The Richard that appears as a human being is an expression of that oneness. The same as the wave in the ocean, Richard is the wave expressing the Christ Consciousness. The seen world is the unreal world, and the unseen world is the real world. For there is not a thing in this material world that matters at all. There is no such thing as old age, or death. As I breathe in I live, as I breathe out I die, for one becomes the other. Balance is the key to all creation. It's the rhythmic balance interchange between two opposites that is the basis of all creation. All questions are answerable on the wave, or cycle.

To know that I and the Father are One, sounds OK. Then if I see the material world as being the effect of that, this sits much better with me, where the fulcrum is between the Father and I, rather than seeing the fulcrum being between the outer world and me.

Because I live in two worlds simultaneous, that is the material world, or the world that I see, and the spiritual world, the unseen world. It is important to have a balanced attitude with the inner world and the outer material world. If I see any differences in the material world, it creates an imbalance out there, which voids itself within me, thus putting me out of balance, and sapping my energy, and restricting me as a true

❧❧

Jesus is not the Christ. He is the way shower. It's
through the teachings of Jesus that I came to
recognise the Christ within, which is where I
became aware that, 'The Father and I are One,'
or God is the Christ consciousness within.

❧❧

expression of who I am. So if I see no issue outside myself, my life flows nicely. I choose never to be positive, or negative, for I see each of these being a limiting factor. Being positive intimates there must be a negative, when no such thing exists. Or to put it another way, if I am positive about something, the balancing effect on the inner is negative. Everything just is.

If I have a problem with somebody, or something, it's an indication that I have separated myself from the oneness of who I am. This perception then becomes a reflection, for all perceptions are reflections, so that I see myself as I truly am. Taking me straight into the illusion, this then sets up a chain of events manifesting in my body as symptoms, which are normally called sickness. These symptoms are all fear based, brought about by resistance to living. Louise Hay has written a wonderful book that outlines how different thought patterns affect certain parts of the body. For example, eye problems arise from, 'not liking what you see in your own life'. Influenza is a response to mass negativity and beliefs. Fear, a belief in statistics. When I see the world around me in balance, I know that I am in balance.

I now know that if I keep my thoughts happy and joyful my body will be healthy. To do this I must stop separating myself from God or the oneness of it all. To do this I need to stop identifying with anything in the material world, or with anything in the body of Richard. Good health is not in my body, but in my consciousness. The cure of the symptom is not in the

❧

A belief that a healer can heal a
sickness supports the belief in sickness,
and the illusion.

❧

body, but in my consciousness.

I need to realize the answer is within the Christ Consciousness. To add strength to this I have found nothing in the material world has any value, whereas in God's world there is an unlimited abundance. For me to realize that I never have to worry about another thing for the rest of my life's journey, is a mind boggling thought? There is nothing I need to do. There is no need for me to pray to God for anything, as I have an abundance of everything I need. My prayer consists of communing with God for guidance only. As I let my pure spirit emanate from within, all will be added unto me.

I picture that beingness, as when I look at a young baby; it shines and portrays pure love. This is the pure Christ Consciousness shining through completely surrendered to a way of openness and innermost vulnerability, not seemingly attached to anything on the outer. That beingness never leaves us. It is my true self, who I really am, which is the one thing we all have in common with each another. It is the power that controls my life, it is where I get all my energy from, as I let all my old beliefs go. As Jesus said "Be as a little child."

As I unfold from my inner beingness, it will permeate to my outer consciousness in such a manner that it will balance all that is. For everything in the universe is in perfect balance. It is only when I identify with anything on the outer that my perception creates the illusion, or imbalance. The ego then takes

❧

Love Without Attachment

After awhile you learn the subtle difference.

Between holding a hand and chaining a soul.

And you learn that love does not mean leaning.

And company does not mean security.

And you begin to learn that kisses are not contracts.

And presents are not promises.

And you begin to accept rejection.

With your head up, and your eyes clear.

With the grace of an adult.

Not the heartache of a child.

And you learn to build your life on now.

Because tomorrow is too uncertain.

After awhile you learn that even sunshine

burns if you get too much.

Plant your garden, and decorate your soul.

Instead of waiting for someone to bring you flowers.

After awhile you learn that you have infinite worth.

❧

over and tries to convince me the illusion is real. If a child throws a ball in the air the universe must adjust to the imbalance this creates. The material world is like a big toy. I can play with it, change it, but I can't fix it. I can get a certain amount of love and joy from it, but nothing of a permanent nature.

A big lesson for me to learn was that this life is not for gratification of self. The ego would have me believe otherwise! It is when I give my attention to anything outside myself; I play the role of the prodigal son, which is being a normal human being. I commit the primary sin of separating myself from the oneness of who I truly am. For I am God in expression. All love and joy come from the Christ consciousness. It cannot be acquired from another person or thing. As a matter of fact I can get nothing from the outer self, or from anyone else. All my ailments are created by me, and can be cured by me. I will never get anything from this world, except the quality of my own being reflected back to me. For I create myself in my own image. The universe is the image and likeness of my consciousness, or my body is expressing exactly my state of consciousness, for the outer is a reflection of the inner.

A good example of this is when I perceive a symptom in the body, which I call sickness; this is the body balancing the minds thinking. So I come back to my inner self and give the symptom no attention at all, for of itself it has no power. All healing must be done at the Christ Conscious level, where the

❦

My purpose here on Earth is to truly focus on
who I am, that is God in expression.

❦

error of thinking occurred. My spirit cannot be controlled by my five senses, my mind, or my emotions, for it just is. My inner beingness, which is the one mind of God, sees no right or wrong, good or bad, everything just is.

So as I keep coming back to this level of thinking, this then becomes habit forming for me, which allows my true self to shine through. To do this I must cease to worry, and let go of all my wants, needs, and beliefs of everything on the outer and rely completely on all the love, joy, and happiness coming from the Christ consciousness within. True love sees no differences, and is total acceptance of all that is.

❧

To treat what I perceive as an illness, it must be done at the Christ Conscious level. For the illness is not in the body, it is in the belief in sickness.

❧

Chapter Two

DO NOT WORRY

Therefore I tell you, do not worry about your life, what you will eat or drink; or about your body, what you will wear. Is not life more important than food, and the body more important than clothes? Look at the birds of the air; they do not sow or reap or store away in barns, and yet your heavenly Father feeds them. Are you not much more valuable than they? Who of you by worrying can add a single hour to his life?

Mathew 6; 25.

The belief that my body needs certain foods is a false belief. Jesus said, "Concern yourself not with what you eat or drink, and be as a sparrow in the field." Because my thoughts are all powerful, when I identify my thoughts with food it throws everything out of balance, first by separating from the oneness, creating a need and a belief that I need certain foods which has a opposite balancing effect on the inner of creating lack. So I am back to creating beliefs again. To clarify this statement, it's my belief that I need to eat healthy food that limits me. I must let go

❦

Any major shift in world consciousness will have to start within me.

❦

my concern for what my diet contains. As I do so the body will let me know when I eat something that it does not like without me telling it what I think it likes. And accept the spiritual truth that the same consciousness that formed the body is now nourishing it, maintaining it, sustaining it, and renewing it unto eternity for it is impossible for me to get any of these from my outer self. For God is my own consciousness appearing as form. This has been a major shift in my thinking. The result of this attitude is that I seem to eat less, and the food passes through me quickly. So nothing matters.

Beliefs mean attachments, which are very limiting factors. To define where I encounter my beliefs, it seems to be always in the material aspect of my daily doings, which is the ego world. When I walk up a steep hill and start to run out of breath, I separate from my true beingness, and lose an enormous amount of energy through my resistance to living. This energy seems to come from the physical body, which is of poor quality. So give it no thought. My ego will try and convince me that I need to exercise and nourish the body with what it thinks all the right foods and vitamins that I should eat. This is fear based because of the feeling of not being well and healthy. Anything, which has a fear base will limit me, and eventually destroy me. As I surrender to all that is, my beingness will take over, then nothing matters at all.

What I choose to do in this life, I choose to do for the

❧

See no more with outer eyes alone, for thou hast
knowing eyes to void the illusions of my sensing.

Walter Russell

oneness of it all. If I identify it with someone or something I bring the ego into it. The body has a wonderful ability to adjust to all it encounters without any input from me. For example if the sun is very bright, I make no comment on this and let the eyes adjust to the problem by never wearing sun glasses, for it's the fear of the sun hurting my eyes that causes the problems. It's the fear of skin cancer that creates the cancer. The fear of skin cancer is not part of my consciousness. The same with mosquito and sand flies. Make no comment on them biting. It is the fear of the mosquito that creates the sting. Just ignore them and the body will adjust to the problem. I never tell myself that I feel tired. If the body gets weary, I lay it down. It seems to sort itself out without any input from me. I never tell myself that I need glasses to read, or my eyes need glasses. I just put them on with no comment. The result is that I hardly ever put my glasses on.

It is all these little acts of not identifying with the outer that create an attitude in my beingness that helps me to stay as one with who I am. So nothing matters.

To get rid of fear from my life, I need to get rid of my resistance to living by letting go my beliefs, for to have a belief is to live in duality, which breeds resistance to living. By dying daily to old beliefs, I eliminate fear from my life. This is what Jesus meant when he said to be born again, let the old ways go, they will not work anymore.

As I live from my true beingness there is no cause and

❦

I create that which I need to learn from. This gives me the mirror image. For the whole world is a reflection of where I am.

❦

effect, this enables me to live a balanced lifestyle in oneness with Christ Consciousness. Even though I am a long way from just being, I feel very excited about the changes that are taking place within me, as doors open up within.

I gave up smoking using the same principle. I realized that smoking was not the problem; it was what I was telling myself, that I felt like or needed a smoke. When I gave no attention to smoking I stopped, never to smoke again. I feel now that if anybody wanted to lose weight, just forget about food and nutrition, for it is not the food that puts the weight on, it's the belief that it does. This belief also builds up saliva in the mouth, which I feel is a big factor in putting on weight. So just let the higher self take over, which it is just waiting to do, if we only let it.

As I let the spiritual world unfold itself to me. I must not be concerned with or disturbed by what is going on in the human world. This does not mean that I put my head in the sand but to go about my affairs doing things according to my highest sense of right. I will have no concern about the results of my efforts. I feel my path now is not to try and improve human conditions but to let the spiritual world unfold as my individual consciousness.

It's all these small acts of letting go, and trust in my beingness to sort it all out that brings me back to 'I and the Father are one.' So now when I go to do something, I question

❧

To me there is only one truth,
'THE FATHER AND I ARE ONE'.

❧

the bottom line. What is my purpose? That is to express the Christ Consciousness from within, and to stay as one with the Father, or the Christ Consciousness, by giving no thought to who may benefit from my actions. If I do this with joy and ecstasy, I seem to have an enormous amount of energy.

To sum this up, if I use ego energy, I am limited to the physical body, but if I tap into the Christ Consciousness I have an unlimited source of energy with a fair bit to spare. This energy will not work for personnel gain.

It is like the one wave in the ocean. The one wave is not capable of sinking a ship, it's all the other waves in the ocean pushing that one wave, which becomes an enormous force. The same applies to the Christ Consciousness, which I am able to tap into. To carry this a step further, if I think I can help anybody or love another person, or give anybody anything, it takes me back to my ego, which creates a lack within based on fear. To overcome this happening, I must keep my focus on my beingness, and give no thought to the recipient. This allows the action being able to void itself in the effect without the ego being involved, which allows the Christ consciousness to flow through me, which is joy, love, help, in its most powerful form. This is the energy that I use. So nothing matters.

The ego will try and convince me there are issues that need changing in the material world, this gives the issue more power, thus creating a bigger problem out there. Instead of me seeing it

❧❧

For me to live completely is to forever rise above my own self during the whole journey of life.

❧❧

as a reflection of something within me that I need to look at. I must realize that everything that happens in my life starts with me and finishes with me; I cannot blame anybody or anything for what happens to me. Nobody can hurt me, make me angry or sad; I cannot even get an illness. I create all these things myself, as I separate myself from my inner self. I then come back to my inner beingness. It is astounding the effect this has on my well being.

The need to care for my physical body is another belief I need to let go, as I come into the state of Christ Consciousness, which knows that the organs and functions of the body have nothing at all to do with my life. It seems all I need to do for exercise, is to practice deep breathing, this creates a cycle, as I breathe in, the cycle is voided by the out breath. The Christ Consciousness has the capability of creating all the nutrients it needs when it needs them without any help from me. All things that I have worried about in my life have been a complete waste of time. For nothing matters, everything just is.

Or the belief that pills and medicine will fix our ailments; they do seem to have an effect, depending how strong our belief is in them. But the real healing comes from the power of the Christ. The ailments that manifest in the body are a belief in sickness in my consciousness, this is where the healing will come from. Consciousness is where God is. As Jesus said, "I of myself do nothing, it is the Father within that doeth the work."

❧

As I give and regive all that I have to give, the more I have to give. For my supply comes from the One Mind. For this is the source of all energy, my physical self has no energy.

❧

My experience with this is, if you need to take pills, do so but give them no attention as you take them. The same with any symptom, give it as little attention as you possibly can. Spiritual illumination does not come from a person, a religion, or sect. It is the illumined consciousness, which dispels the sense of the ego, with its ills, and failures. This is another example of the body having no power to be able to destroy itself. In my opinion it's the separation from the 'I And The Father Are One,' which is the cause of all the sickness and the problems in the world today. For this is the ultimate truth.

As I surrender to my inner beingness, there will an awakening taking place, a kind of flow of awareness. There will be a feeling of love without identity in being a loving person, for love cannot come from another. Whatever this love touches it will heal. This will be my true self, shining through. We all have this true beingness that has not changed one bit since the day we were born.

This true self will only shine through when I am absolutely honest with who I am. It can do this if I have no thought, belief, need, or want. This attitude has taken me some time to fully understand. When I see a need to make the world a better place to live in, or try and help somebody, it creates a lack within, which in turn creates a lack in the mass consciousness of the universe, because of the sheer power of my thoughts. The only way is for me to see the whole universe as being in perfect

❧

The continuation of creation is based upon the constant giving of one half of a cycle to the other half for the purpose of repeating the creative process through another cycle of giving for regiving.

The Divine Iliad

❧

balance this means staying as one with the Christ Consciousness within. For I And The Father Are One. For this is who I Am. Nothing matters.

An ancient Chinese sage states that, "If you are planning a year ahead, sow a seed. If you are planning ten years ahead, plant a tree. If you are planning one hundred years ahead, educate the people."

Chapter Three

GOOD HEALTH

When I was fifty six years old, I finished up out of work, so for the first time in my life had a good look at myself. My health was in a shocking state. I was bleeding from the bowel, and had been for about ten years, getting worse all the time; a heavy smoker, with a shocking cough, constipated, and worst of all with a crook back that the experts told me was incurable. They even suggested that I get an invalid pension. The back I believed was caused by thirty years of heavy lifting in the saw milling industry.

It was at this time that I had a big shift in my thinking. The back problem was not caused by heavy lifting. It was only my belief that this was the problem. All my other symptoms I treated the same way, without the use of doctors, diet, or medicine. So after about ten years of meditating and study, now at the age of seventy five I enjoy excellent health, with an abundant amount of energy, and some to spare. The healing coming from getting rid of old beliefs, and changing my attitude of mind.

❦

"God does not give material things without your equal regiving, for that is the inviolate law regarding all material things."

HSC Course

❦

I asked myself the question, how would I handle a serious illness? First it would give me a wonderful opportunity to change my thinking, and beliefs as I have created this illness, I must be able to cure it from within. If I give the symptom any attention, it will empower it, the body is not capable of sustaining an illness of its self. So far as the doctors and their treatment is concerned I would work with them 100%. But give as little attention as possible to the symptoms and the medicine that they prescribe

I choose to no longer be on a spiritual path, as this leads me deeper into the illusion of trying to get a better way of living, which is a very ego orientated path to follow. I choose to no longer lead the life of a human being, as this limits me also and separates me from God. For too long I have been leading the life of the prodigal son. I now realize I am a spiritual being, having a spiritual experience.

Also my beingness is not the body of Richard, but in the Christ Consciousness. There is no spiritual growth to be gained from the five senses. It's OK for me to enjoy these, but to expect no growth from them.

It is very apparent to me now that the old ways will not work any more, where I will love you, if you will love me; I will give you this, if you give me that. I must now 'Live Inside Out.' And become a co-creator with all that is, not a manipulator of life. The only way I can get anything for myself is to become the

All the power that man has is in his knowing.

For every person must know himself.

fulcrum by giving that which has been given to me by God so that it may be re-given again to the oneness, without any attachment to that which I give. This voids the cycle. Love and joy do not come from another person, or from Richard, it comes from God. This is why relationships don't work very well, for love must emanate from the soul level where all is one. Creating is a true expression of my Christ Consciousness, which is forever unfolding, disclosing and revealing itself as my individual consciousness.

The beauty is in the universe reflecting who I am. God is the universe, and I, Richard am an expression of that universe.

As I come to grips with the material world, I realize the only illusionary part of it is my perception of it. I liken it to the story told of a man who got out of his bath and stepped on a bit of rope on the floor, thinking it was a snake. Horror overcame him and he shook with fear, anticipating in his thoughts all the agonies caused by a serpent's venomous bite. What a relief it is when he sees that the rope is no snake. The cause of his fright lies in his ignorance of the illusion.

I cannot meet a problem on the level of the problem. I must rise above the level of appearance in order to bring out the harmony of being. For my real existence is as Spirit. It's only in

❧

Pain is nothing but resistance to the God
energy caused by fear.
Without fear and resistance, death would
be a transition to another dimension.

❧

the degree that I perceive my real existence as Spirit that I drop my false sense of life as material person. The spiritual world is the unseen half of the cycle, the material world being the other half of the same cycle. It is my ability to balance this cycle that enables me to maintain a quality of lifestyle. The one basic law of all God's creation is the 'Rhythmic Balance Interchange' between balanced opposites. Such as positive and negative, male and female, compression and expansion, buyer and seller, and a countless other division of ideas, each voids itself in the other. 'Every action or thought has a balanced opposite reaction' and must void itself in the expression.

What I fear the most is what I will attract. What I resist will persist. The illness that I suffer has no power of itself; the illness survives and multiplies on the fear that I feed it. It is my considered opinion that no illness can kill us of itself. The fear that I generate within is the destructive force. It's this fear of what this illness can do that causes death. The more I feed the fear the more power the illness has to develop into a life threatening disease.

This old parable sums it up. A Native American grandfather was talking to his grandson about how he felt. He said, "I feel as if I have two wolves fighting in my heart. One wolf is the vengeful, angry, violent one. The other wolf is the loving, compassionate one." The grandson asked him, "Which wolf will win the fight in your heart?" The grandfather answered, "The

❦

Honour all religions,

each one is a pathway to the one God.

❦

one I feed."

The supremacy of man is dependent upon the measure of his ability to live knowingly in the undivided Mind universe. The master makes use of the divided universe of sensed-matter as he wills — or dismisses it from his Consciousness when he wills. Until you become master of matter, it will master you.

❦

The universe is in perfect balance, and reveals
as much of itself as we can see.

❦

Chapter Four

INSIGHTS

Last year I had two insights that I need to write down and clarify. The first one was when I was working in Marie and Herman's garden at Nerang. Marie had given me some pansies to plant. After they had been in for about ten days I was 'tickling' around them, that is moving the soil around them, as all plants love this sort of attention. It was a gorgeous day, clear blue sky, birds trying to outdo one another with their songs. It was so peaceful. Then a powerful thought hit me. "You are the garden Richard." I sat down suddenly and thought, how true. So with this insight I shifted my attention from how well the plants were doing, to the quality of the soil. The result was the plants seemed to respond with lush growth. Then as I shifted my focus further back in the chain of events to where I am consciously expressing my soul to the fullest in balance with God, I experienced the most beautiful feeling of peace from within. The sheer wonder, joy and abundance that I get from expressing my pure beingness from within leaves all other methods lacking.

❧

No man gives of himself but himself, and no man
takes away from himself but himself.

❧

The next insight was even more powerful, it happened in Geraldine's garden on Mount Tamborine about six months later. I was weeding her rose garden, all was very still, there was no one about, and the birds were again very active. I had a powerful flash, which lasted a fraction of a second. I saw a human being in a fetal position with no clothes on. The message this time was all powerful, it said: "All humans are one hundred percent pure love." I didn't sleep that night as I pondered this insight. I have now come to the conclusion why this is so, for we are one hundred percent love. As this is who we are on the spiritual level, it stands to reason if we can express this unconditional love in the material world it would be our greatest strength. Nothing could destroy or hurt us. So nothing matters.

This one hundred percent pure love that we are is that state of true beingness which emanates from that small child within that I need to let show forth from within me. This love sees no good or bad, right or wrong, trauma or happiness. It is completely non-judgmental. There is nothing I need to do for this to happen. It just is. I must realize that I cannot use my conscious mind or any of my senses to attain a state of beingness, for this would lead to an untrue way to express the Christ Consciousness.

Man is dependent solely upon his transformation from being an outer-sensing body to becoming an inner-knowing Mind. This also means that there can never be a spiritual rebirth

❦

God makes a way where there is no way.

❦

of man until he has first become transformed by the discovery of his inner-self unity with God.

❧

"*Our concept of knowledge has been built upon the complexity of multitudinous effect instead of the utter simplicity of the cause of complex effect. Cause is as simple as the three mirrors in a kaleidoscope, while effect is as complex as the infinite repetition of a few pieces of broken glass reflected within those three mirrors.*"

HSC, Science of Man

❧

Chapter Five

I AND THE FATHER ARE ONE

At night in my quite moments, just before going to sleep, I choose to ask for guidance. By communing with God. Explaining that I am His expression, willing and able to do His work whenever, and wherever. This triggered off a whole new line of thought, and insights which I felt guided to write down. It seems to me now that what I need to awaken to must come from within me. Teachers and books have only a triggering effect, when the student is ready, the teacher will appear.

It was quiet a turnaround last night when I asked for guidance. I asked myself why I still chose to be a human being, having a spiritual experience. Why couldn't I be a spiritual being having a spiritual experience? This set me to thinking; if I could do this it would overcome all the lack and frailties of being a human being.

Then it came to me to see the concept of 'The Father and I Are One', in reverse. That is, 'Richard is one With Me'. I am his (Richard's) supply and will give him everything that he needs or

❦

"No matter what you must do in life, do it joyously. Whatever work it is, put love into it. If you do put love into it, you will find love regiven to you by it. Love given out from you vitalizes you as well as it vitalizes the one you give it to."

HSC Course, The Science of Man

❦

wants forever and ever. His joy in re-giving the abundance that I have given him will be beyond his wildest dreams. But he must stay as one with Me. Providing Richard abides by the laws that I have set down when I created him in my image, he will enjoy an abundance of all he desires, and good health forever.

Another way of coming to grips with this way of thinking, is to see Me as the cause of all that is, he then becomes the fulcrum to express that abundance. It is in the fulcrum where the power is. All My creations are in perfect balance. Richard is coming to realize that I am his father, and all supply and energy comes from within Me, and that I have much to offer that he knows not of. The one basic law that he must abide by is that he must love Me with all his heart and soul, and to love his neighbors as himself. 'For I am love'. And his neighbor is himself.

He cannot hurt his neighbor without hurting himself, he cannot love his neighbor without loving himself. His desire to love his neighbor is in balance with his ability to love himself. He must remain in balance with My law of Rhythmic Balance Interchange.

Richard's days of being a prodigal son are over. He need no longer act the role of a human being, he is now a one hundred percent spiritual being. If Richard thinks he can go off and help his friends, he is doing them a dis-service, as he separates himself from Me. His service is illusionary. To make matters worse for him, when he thinks he is helping his friends, he has only the

❦

As I let go my conventional thinking, doors open
up like when I let my beliefs go.

☾☽

energy of a human being. But when he comes back to Me I will give him an unlimited amount of soul energy which he knows not of, this soul energy cannot be used for personnel, material gain, or serve a selfish end. But only for the soul to express. For all supply and energy must come from Me. For Richard and I are one. The only real way he can help his friends is to show them where he gets his supply of abundance, health, energy and balance. This would be showing real gratitude. For what I the Father has to offer cannot be taught, it must be awakened from within, and lived.

As Richard was a prodigal son for so many of his lifetimes, it will take some time for him to come to grips with being a spiritual being. He looks out at the material world, which I have created, and thinks it is very real. But his perception of the material world will be very illusionary, for he sees only one half of the cycle, which is the material world, the other half being the spiritual world. This limits him, which is the case with all humans. He will be unable to see the perfect balance and abundance that I have created. When he identifies with anything in that world thinking he can gain something from it, he will limit himself. And he will create a lack within, for my law of balance must prevail, which says, the degree that what he seeks on the outer will have a balanced and opposite effect as lack within.

All of the good necessary for his welfare will be supplied to

❝❞

Gandhi said, "be the change
that you want to become."

❝❞

him in greater abundance than he can accept when he gives up the desire to get, achieve, accomplish, or seek gratification as Richard practices giving and re-giving of himself without attachment, he need take no thought for his own well being. When he does this the more energy he will have. The same thing applies when he lets go of his attachments to any material possessions, and lets go of all his needs and wants, for while he hangs on to these he creates and enormous lack within which in turn affects the consciousness of the whole universe, creating more lack, and starvation. Oh what a wonderful way of living.

' Therefore I tell you, do not worry.'

As I have been created by the Father in His image. It gives me great pleasure to become aware of the wonder of it all. I have been given a body, which is perfect in every way, so that I may express fully the Oneness of all creation. I liken myself to a light bulb; until it is switched on it cannot reflect the light, which comes from its source. The pure love that I am is a never-ending expression of awakening from within.

I have been given many surface vehicles for my use. The five senses, intuition, emotion, affection, laughter, joy, abundant energy. All to be used for my expression of who I AM. My gratification in this life will come from my expression of who I Am, as I re-give the abundance that I have been given to re-give. If I feel I need more than I have been given, it will cause a lack within me, which will limit who I am. I have been given an ego

❧

The paradoxical Buddhist insight is that to reach the other shore from this shore, one must come from the other shore.

❧

as a surface vehicle, which has created the illusion that I may see a reflection of myself in what it tries to convince me is the material world. The ego will do everything with the power that I give it to convince me that illusion is real. This will confuse me to the point of my own destruction.

However, if I accept the ego as being a necessary tool to guide me on my progress, and to see the mirror effect of how I am going, this will then lead me to a total acceptance to all that is and thereby become a perfect expression of who I truly am.

The black boy and the white boy were discussing whether Jesus was a white man or a black man.

"I bet you a dollar he is white." Says the white boy.

"Ah bet you a dollar he ain't white." Replies the black boy.

"But how is we gonna find out?"

"Easy, we will just pray to him, and ask."

So they prayed, and voice came back that said.

"I am what I am."

"There you go, I told you he is white, give me your dollar."

"Hang on a bit, how does that make him white?"

"Had he been black, he would have said, 'I is what I is.

❧

To learn the path of enlightenment is to learn the self. To learn the self is to forget the self. To forget the self is to be enlightened by the whole. To be enlightened by the whole is to let the body and mind of oneself and those of others drop away. Then no trace of enlightenment remains. The traceless enlightenment continues to advance forever more.

Yasuhico Kimura, *Think Kosmically Act Globally*

❧

Chapter 6

THERE IS NO ILLUSION

It took me a long time to come to grips with how a loving God could be so cruel as to create so much suffering in the world. The penny dropped for me when I heard three prominent men discuss the problems in the world and how they thought they could be solved. One was a Catholic Priest, another a Church of England Minister, and the third a Sai Baba representative. The Catholic Priest spoke of the enormous problems that needed to be overcome and went on to list the starvation and poverty he saw in the third world countries. The Anglican Minister agreed with him and said, "But we must all work together to solve these problems that confront all of us". The Sai Baba representative said, "I disagree with both of you. There are no problems out in the world, they are all within man himself, and that's where we will solve them."

It has now dawned on me that the illusion is not out in the material world, but in my consciousness, created there by my senses deceiving me into believing something that is not true.

❦

Inner freedom comes when I cease to
identify with anything that is not me.

Because I identify with nothing, I am
everything.

Yasuhico Kimura

❧

My senses can only perceive the one half of the cycle, which is the material world, the other half of the cycle being the spiritual world, or the unseen world.

My senses tell me that the sun is hot and will cause skin cancer, this then sets up a belief that actually creates the cancer, so it's not the sun that is the cause of skin cancer, but the belief that it is so. My senses tell me that the mosquito bite stings, so this sets up a belief that mosquitoes sting; it's not the mosquito that causes the sting, but my belief that it is so. It's my belief that I need money that causes the lack of it in my life. I use money but I don't need it, for it's only a medium of exchange and will always be there to use. And so it goes on as I get rid of these beliefs that are part of my consciousness that I think are real, but are really all an illusionary part of my consciousness. My senses are like my body they can know nothing and have no power at all, not even to sustain an illness. If I take notice of my senses and feelings I am being dishonest with myself, and I will never see that innermost beauty that remains deep within me. When I express from my inner beingness, there is no right or wrong, good or bad. All suffering is caused by separation from God. For it's when I identify with anything in the material world that my perception becomes illusionary.

The concept that we have many lifetimes sits well with me. Before I incarnate each time it seems that I will select my parents who will conceive me, I will choose my moment of birth, my

❧

God is no-body

God is no-thing

God is.

or

I Am no-body

I Am no-thing

I Am.

❧

date of birth, and my own name. I will have written a script for my journey through this lifetime, bringing into my journey all those experiences that will help me become as one with God, for it is in the traumas of life that I experience the greatest growth. If I don't do too good this lifetime I will get plenty more opportunities in the coming lifetimes.

Recently I watched a documentary on Henry Kissenger the Secretary of State of America during the Vietnam War. It showed how he was responsible for the slaughter of millions of Vietnam civilians. This upset me greatly, as I pondered on this for a couple of days. Then it dawned on me that in other lifetimes I would have done similar things, I would have been a child rapist, murderer, all those horrible things on my journey of oneness with God. So who am I to be judgmental of anybody?

I must give in to win. For there never has been and never will be an issue worth fighting for in this life. To be truly free of any outcome from any situation is to live my life in balance. There is nothing that I need, because everything is presently complete. Nothing in this material universe is what it appears to be, for my senses deceive me. Everything just Is. It's that inner beingness, the Christ Consciousness that governs all the functions of my body and the universe. If I as a spiritual being get into the habit of tapping into this oneness, I will never need to suffer again.

I liken this oneness to all the trees and plants on the earth.

❦

*Whether humanity is to continue and
comprehensively prosper on spaceship earth
depends entirely on the human individual and
not on the political and economic systems.*

Buckminster Fuller

❦

They have their roots in the soil, which is connected to all the soil on the earth. Each plant is connected to each other through the soil. The same applies to the ocean, as all the oceans are connected as one, as is each wave connected to every ocean. I as a spiritual being am also connected to the oneness which is the Christ Consciousness which is God.

Jesus made two statements that had a dynamic effect in my life. In the Beatitudes he said, "Resist not an evil person." The other one was, "Give it no thought." Give no thought to that with which you clothe your body, give no thought to what you eat or drink, give no thought to the morrow, be as a little child, or as a sparrow in the field.

To me the resurrection that Jesus spoke of is the dying daily of the old beliefs and being born again to the new concept that the Father and I Are One. I see this as the second coming of Christ, as I realize the Christ within. Richard has risen from the human ways and human beliefs to be replaced by absolute faith in the abundance of all that is, having no need for any beliefs whatsoever. There is no such thing as suffering.

As I let go of living in duality, by dying daily, I eliminate fear from my life. Also there is no cause and effect for cause is effect; one becomes the other, the same as life and death, for one is the other. I live to die and die to live. As I breathe in I live, as I breathe out I die. My body is dying every moment and is continually changing moment by moment.

❧

If I could be as a sparrow in the field and have no thought, I would be everybody and everything.

❧

This enables me to live a balanced lifestyle in oneness with Christ Consciousness. Even though I am a long way from just 'being,' I feel very excited about the changes that are taking place within me, as I open to the oneness of all creation. As I see the good in my neighbor, this builds me up, which then builds up the whole world.

The writing of this book has helped me enormously in clarifying my thoughts as a new awakening is taking place within, this last week particularly as a bigger shift in consciousness has taken place.

This very basic principle of looking at the outside world and seeing it as very real, and realizing the illusion is in my consciousness. All my problems have been created by my perception of where the illusion is. All beliefs are illusionary, and fear based, and separates me from God, or the oneness of it all. Everything in creation is in perfect balance. Nothing matters.

It's not my role to change the world, but I feel it's my role to change my own consciousness, which in turn changes the world. Every individual in the world has the potential to change the world into a better place from within himself. For we as spiritual beings, have been given dominion over all creation.

A wise man does not centre his attention upon effects. They are to him as the ashes. The fire of the original spirit is ever new and fresh he does not identify himself with the ashes.

❦

My Father and I are One

❦

Chapter Seven

As a Man Thinketh

I liken this to growing a garden. To grow a good garden, I would select a nice bit of soil, in a sunny spot, I would remove all the weeds and rubbish, fertilize it with some good manure, dig this in, then water it, plant the corn, peas and beans. It would then depend how well I tended that garden as to what sort of crop it produced.

The same principle applies to my consciousness. If I get rid of all my old beliefs and limited thinking, fertilize the mind with good thoughts, then depending how well I tend those thoughts, this would govern the quality of my life.

All creation is based upon the constant giving of one half of a cycle to the other half of a cycle for the purpose of repeating the creative process through another cycle of giving for re-giving. One half of the cycle is for compression, which is the thought, or the unseen part of the cycle. The other half is for expansion, which is the expression, or the effect part of the cycle. As each finds rest in the other, they constantly void one

Every right is balanced by a wrong

another. This is the law of balance, where all energy comes from. Compression in an engine is balanced by an equal expansion. As a man starts to walk he takes one step which puts him out of balance so he takes another step to come back to balance.

The law of love is absolute. It bears no relation to religion, sin, good or evil. Love is the desire to give. It is the cause of all effect. The effect has no reality, it must void itself in the oneness. Cause alone is. As I express my beingness, I must give no thought to the effect. As Jesus said, have no thought. To give any thought to the effect would take me back into my ego, which thrives on duality.

As I get into the habit of working from my true inner beingness I will be guided into making the best decisions for my well being. I call it living inside out. The bottom line is not so much to cure the illness, for the cure will come from my consciousness as I come to realize who I am, a divine spiritual being. By giving the symptom no attention, or power, it will be unable to survive, and will eventually disappear. As Jesus said, give it no thought.

Everything that happens in my life I have created for a purpose to help and guide me into becoming as one with God. I create all the accidents that happen, all my illnesses. The people that I bring into my life are also for me to learn more about myself. Every person presents a mirror image of myself. When I see something in another person that I don't like, it's a mirror of

✿

*I think as many negative
thoughts as I think positive
thoughts. For one is the other.*

✿

a fault in me. This is a difficult one for me to come to grips with. It is also an indication that I have difficultly in accepting myself. My ego constantly tells me it's the other person who should change, not me. The more traumas that I experience, is a strong and powerful message for me to change my thinking.

I have experienced enormous spiritual growth by recognizing the faults I see in another as being the same faults that are within myself. As I become aware of this, doors have opened that were never opened before. It has been an enormous stepping stone for me to come to this awareness. I can now see the other person as a divine being and am able to totally accept them as they are. For me total acceptance is true unconditional love, which is just Being.

My thoughts are the most powerful force in the world. For they create all that happens in my world — the good — the sickness — joy — harmony — happiness. I cannot get an illness. I cannot catch an illness from somebody. The most common cause of any illness is separation from God, which allows fear, or lack within to manifest. I see myself as playing the role of the prodigal son, as I separate myself from oneness of it all. There is but one teacher, nature, this includes all creation. For all intelligence, knowledge and power are the divine inheritance of everyone.

It is an illusion to think that knowledge comes from reading books, or that I can acquire it from teachers. The greatest

☙❧

There is only one soul expressing as many.

☙❧

teachers in the world, the philosophers, geniuses, can only impart information. The senses can observe and record, but they cannot know, for thinking is not knowing. All knowledge must come from the Christ Consciousness, which is the higher self.

I once heard a Taoist define a teacher. He said, "A teacher is one who will awaken in the student that which the student already knows." As I tap into the One Mind — my beingness, or Christ Consciousness, which is where I see God as being. All knowledge comes from this source. I don't need to do anything to be. Nothing matters, but thinking makes it so. It is impossible for anyone to be separate from God. It's only my belief that creates the illusion that I am separate. This is the source of all my problems. in the same way it's impossible for the wave to be separate from the ocean. As I live the life of a spiritual being having a spiritual experience, I see no good or bad, right or wrong, harmony or disharmony. If I could live the life of oneness with God, I would never suffer an illness. For everything just is.

Fear creates a resistance to living, which restricts me and limits me being who I am. When I let my emotions express fear, anger, jealously, and hatred, the body starts to move in the direction that destroys the body. These sensations multiply the acid elements and destroy the body by developing toxic conditions, which ultimately promotes various destructive growths, which gradually decay the body until it is destroyed.

❧❧

Striving for more confesses to being less.

❧❧

Chapter 8

THE VEGETABLE GARDEN

I had a strong desire for many years to grow a vegetable garden and sell them at a roadside stall. I did not really know why I had this urge but it was just something that I needed to do. The opportunity came when I mentioned it to Keith and Jean whom I had known for some time. They have a seven acre property at Cudgen in northern New South Wales. They suggested that I could use their land to grow the garden, free of charge. It was also at this time that I had just finished reading a book by Neale Donald Walsh, called New Revelations. In it his main message to me was that we all need to look at our beliefs. He was referring mainly to the churches, so I chose to have a look at my beliefs.

I decided to live in my Coaster bus on site near the veggie garden as this seemed to give me the ideal setup to tune into the oneness of it all. It became very apparent to me at the beginning that what I was trying to establish within with myself was the oneness with the garden and myself. Each night I would ask for

❧

Anything that pertains to duality
is attachment to suffering.

❧

guidance on all the unanswered questions that were being presented to me as I let my beliefs go. Doors opened that had been closed, that revealed who I was.

Looking back in hindsight I can remember when I went to see Sai Baba in India in 1990. In the aeroplane on takeoff from Madras I heard a voice so loud and clear said to me, 'Know Who You Are.' The mind boggling thought that came to me was that the universe has but one creator — one mind, one person, one being. We are that creator, that Person, that Being in the measure that we know we are. I don't have to do anything to be who I am, for my true self is my inner beingness. To be nobody is to be that oneness of it all.

One of my main awakenings was to realize that 'The garden is me expressing who I AM.' Everything that I see in the world is me expressing myself. For the universe is me expressing who I am. We are all one, we are all one another. To realize this makes it impossible to do anything for self, for whatever I do will be for the whole or oneness of it all. This would seem to eliminate the ego, which seems to rule the senses.

I gave a lady some veggies that I had grown and explained to her that the veggies were me expressing who I am. When she explained to her husband at dinner that night what I had said, his reply was, "That means we must be eating Richard for dinner tonight." So nothing matters.

As I changed from being a manipulator of the garden to a

❧

My senses are useless when it
comes to understanding perception.

❧

co-creator, I found that it wasn't the grubs in the tomatoes that were the problem, but my attitude. So realizing the garden and I were one, the grubs seemed to change their attitude also. Instead of talking to the veggies, I tuned into the spirituality of them. I was guided to use a pyrethrum spray in very light applications The message that seemed to come to me was that it wasn't the spray that kept the pests at bay, but my desire to be the garden.

This got me to thinking how could this be so, as I continued to ask for guidance from within. Each night I would pray to the Father within (Christ Consciousness) and ask for guidance; my prayer did not consist of words but more of a communion with my higher self. For all knowledge is within. The message I got was that all creation is a vibration, at different levels of consciousness. That nature is the living expression of the Universal Thinker, the Christ Consciousness. By being in tune with The One Mind it is able to change the frequency of the vibrations whatever it is in tune with. This is a difficult concept to come to grips with. I would liken it to the ability of the Christ, which is the spirit that animated Jesus to heal the sick. (The Christ is not the Jesus of two thousand years ago). The balance of His pure beingness would have altered the vibration of the patient to such a degree that the illness could not be maintained.

It's a similar thing with cancer patients, many believe that cancer needs an acid body to survive, whereas in an alkaline

❦

*My abundance will not come
from what I have I created.   But
from within myself, the Oneness.*

❧

body cancer cannot survive, which is a different vibration. It would seem to me that the fear of cancer causes the acid build up in the body. Eliminate fear, and this would allow the body to become more alkaline in content. The food we eat has nothing to do with the acid build up in the body.

Another way of looking at this is if I give an abundance of love and joy into growing the veggies, they will flourish in direct proportion to my ability to be the garden, for the garden cannot be outside of me, and I cannot be outside the garden. They would balance that by re-giving an abundance of lovely vegetables in return. There would be a balance of equal interchange between opposite conditions manifesting the love principal of balance upon which God's universal body is founded. It's not unlike if I tuned a thousand violins alike and sound one note on one of them, all will start sounding the same note.

I must let all beliefs of right and wrong go, for one is the other. The same with balanced opposites; cause is effect, negative is positive, good is bad, and bad is good. I even create my own reaction immediately I observe something, for creation is made up of waves of frequencies; one half the wave is toward God, the other half is away from God. Each is as powerful as the other, the real power is at the fulcrum, for this is where God is, forever centering from within and controlling from without simultaneously. There is nothing in the universe that is separate

❧

*The ultimate end of my journey
will be right where it began -
here and now.*

❧

from the oneness.

I experienced wonderful growth in my inner awareness when I worked with Evelyn, for a period of ten years, as a gardener on her spiritual retreat, Rumbalara, on Tamborine Mountain creating a Garden of Eden. We both became aware that the faults that we saw in the other were a reflection of our own individual faults. A further awakening came when I saw her expressing me who I am. Therefore she has no faults, which means I totally accept who she is. The next awareness was to realize she just is. There is nothing outside of self to accept. By operating from this level of consciousness there is no blame, for I take full responsibility for what I perceive is happening in my life knowing full well that I created all that is happening. I also noticed that when I was balanced, Evelyn was great to get along with. For I and The Father are One. So nothing matters.

In the growing of the vegetable garden on Keith and Jean's land at Cudgen, it became obvious that nature is the one teacher, the universe is a living spiritual body of energy in motion, which embraces us all, including plant life and everything in the universe. I now need to learn and know about the spirituality of all nature. For I am the creator of all that is.

My Energy does not come from the physical body, but from the desire of mind to express and create with joy and ecstasy. Desire creates its own power. The energy and motivating force, which creates the universe, is not in matter, nor in motion.

❧❧

*It's my belief in sickness and
pain that creates my attachment
to suffering.*

❧❧

temporary solution, this is only the effect of the problem. The cure would be to overcome an error in my consciousness. The same would apply to a heavy smoker. To get a permanent cure is not in the ability to stop smoking, but to realize it's that the person is telling the consciousness that it needs to smoke. When he stops telling himself that he feels like a smoke, it will be impossible to smoke.

All the problems and traumas that happen in my life are in my consciousness and are cured from my ability to come back to the Oneness of it all. To do this I need to let go and let God. There is nothing outside of self.

I have a strong desire to live this philosophy that I have written and to get the full benefit it must be expressed in my daily living. In so living it, more will be revealed to me. What I have experienced so far, my well being and sheer joy of living makes my life very exciting.

Evelyn and I are both dragons in the Chinese astrology, and when we first started working together there was a strong conflict between us on which way a job should be done. Finally Evelyn said to me, "Look Richard, there is an old saying that says, 'if one horse can pull so much, two horses pulling together will pull eight times as much,' so let's try doing that, by working together." This we did, and it was amazing how much more we got done. From that point on we never put the other down but always added to what the other had suggested.

❦

*I can never suffer illness or
traumas in my life when I know
who I am.*

❦

Energy is solely a mind force. So when I do anything now I choose to do it joyously, and I chose to love what I am doing no matter what. This gives me an excess of energy for my needs without having to take pills, exercise, diet etc. This attitude then goes into the Christ Consciousness, which then affects the whole universe. There is no task in which I manifest God, which is not beautiful, if I make it so. If I do not like my work, it does not like me. The surest way to prevent myself from getting anything for myself is to seek it for myself. For I must now learn to lose myself in order to find my Universal Self. This universe is entirely spiritual. God alone is.

Evelyn's father, Bill has been one of my greatest teachers, it was on his 90th birthday (he is now 95) that he said, "There is no such thing as old age, or death, it's all in the mind." With this attitude he has lived a life without having to go into a hospital. His ability to be very active so late in life has been wonderful for me to see. I was working with him on Evelyn's property fixing the guttering on the roof of her house. We were up and down ladders all day. By about three o'clock I was feeling a bit exhausted, and I was twenty years younger than Bill, so was pleased when he said, "Let's knock off now Richard, we have done a good days work, I will sleep well tonight." He made a point of never saying he was tired, but that he just needed to recharge his batteries. If my body were overweight, the problem would not be to try and lose weight for this would only be a

❦

I cannot become as one with the Father while I live two truths.

I must live the one truth to be fully maintained and sustained from within.

❦

I also noticed that when Evelyn was pleasant to me, I was more balanced. I noticed the same thing in the garden; that when I got excited and enthusiastic about the way the veggies were growing, they seemed to respond in a like manner, or the other way around! This then would indicate that by working as one, the energy is multiplied eight times…

❧

*The reward for the writing of
this book will not come from any
money it may generate,*

*but from the awakening of the
soul within me,*

to who I Am.

❧

Epilogue

Having spent the last twelve months putting this book together, my thoughts are starting to come to grips with the awakening that there can only be this moment to live, no past, no future, only now. For all cause and effect are simultaneous, the same as living and dying, for one is the other. This line of thought would overcome the mystery of no beginning and the no end. This then would enable me to live just in the moment, which is utter bliss, where nothing will ever matter...

Richard.

Made in the USA
Charleston, SC
05 January 2012